A Sixth Grader's Journey to the Great Southern Land

A Sixth Grader's Journey to the Great Southern Land

Arnav Gupta

EXCELLER BOOKS®
A GLOBAL PRESS

A Sixth Grader's Journey to the Great Southern Land

Edited by Prof. (Dr) Kum Kum Ray

Cover by Exceller Books using resources from Pixabay.com

ISBN: 978-93-48892-17-1

Published in India in 2025 by Exceller Books,
An imprint of GE Group,
G1, Dream Apartment, Degree College Road, Belgharia,
Kolkata, 700056, India
www.excellerbooks.com

EXCELLER BOOKS®
A GLOBAL PRESS

My Dadi (Grandma)

Foreword

I, a grandmother glittering with pride, am writing a Foreword for the narratives by our first grandson, Arnav Gupta. A precious divine gift to Dr Rai Umapati Ray, IPS, and Prof (Dr) Kum Kum Ray, and to the closely linked joint family of the Gorakhpur Rai/Ray landlord lineage, continuing the traditions. The first son of our brilliant, dedicated, hardworking, diligent Hewitt Gold Medallist of King George's Medical College (KGMC), Lucknow — Dr Mahoua Ray — is presently settled in Kansas, USA, and is a frequent traveller, taking her sons for worldwide exposure.

The following pages, written by Arnav Gupta, were shared with me years ago. He was 11 back then. It is my heart-warming reward to see this book, A Sixth Grader's Journey to the Great Southern Land – with pictures, on his visit to Australia, published for perspectives of youngsters to be taken seriously by seniors, and also for psychologists and parents to learn from the words written by an eleven-year-old Indian boy born in the US, still conversing and sharing with his grandmother in India. Heart-warming wishes to all readers.

Prof. (Dr.) Kum Kum Ray
Director, Amity School of Languages
Amity University Uttar Pradesh Lucknow Campus
UP, India

About the Author

Arnav Gupta is a 12-year-old who enjoys playing golf competitively, swimming, and playing football and cricket for fun. He has been to 13 countries with his family and is a big foodie. In his free time, he enjoys reading and playing as much golf as he can. He lives in Lenexa, Kansas, with his family. He visited Australia in May 2019 after finishing his fifth grade at Barstow School. He hand-typed the book and shared it with his grandmother.

Acknowledgments

I would like to thank my family, particularly my Mom, for pushing me to do this so much. I would also like to thank everyone in Brisbane for being so friendly and for helping us get settled. Finally, to my younger brother, Darsh, for being so understanding. Another thanks to all my grandparents. Nani (Mom's mom), Nana (Mom's dad), Baba (Dad's Dad) & Dadi (Dad's Mom). Then, a final thank you to my parents for making this possible.

Arnav Gupta
Lenexa Kansas
July 17, 2019

Contents

- One -
Arrival in Brisbane

It was 4:30 a.m. on a winter morning in Brisbane. It had been three days since the last day of school on May 18. In those three days, I had travelled halfway around the world—from my family's house in the suburbs of Kansas City to Brisbane International Airport on the Gold Coast of Australia. My dad had been invited to speak at the World Congress of Pain. It was a worldwide conference held every two years. He was invited to discuss his research and conclusions on how to treat pain caused by a stimulator injection. This year, it was in Sydney, and he decided to take advantage of the opportunity and have a vacation in Australia with the whole family.

First, we were in Brisbane for two nights, staying with one of my mum's childhood friends. She had a daughter my age and a dog that played with us constantly, though she was already at school when we arrived. After breakfast, we went to the koala sanctuary, which baffled me since all the animals were in small cages and were starving. My tip is to avoid this place whenever you are in Brisbane. Do not feed the will to keep treating these animals so poorly. The only good part was hugging the koala. After the encounter, we headed to the café to grab meat for the kangaroos, though they seemed too shy to come and get it.

Here's a tip: if you go to Brisbane, Moreton Island is a must-see. It is the third-largest sand island in the world. Unfortunately, our family was unable to go there. We then headed to eat at Patina at Customs House. A word of advice—be on your best behaviour, because people there complain frequently. My younger brother, Darsh, was speaking loudly, so the table next to us complained every five minutes. One man at the table was cursing under his breath. Towards the end of our meal, we spotted a huge transparent ball with chairs inside, and we enjoyed ourselves.

Then I arrived at Usana Auntie's house (my mum's childhood friend). I collapsed into bed and fell fast asleep. I woke up in the middle of the night, and then Gori woke up and introduced herself. After some time, everyone slowly woke up. Then everybody had breakfast—boiled eggs and some cereal—and Gori went to band practice before school. Then Usana Auntie's personal trainer came in for a routine workout. I joined and did some drills for a while.

After that, we headed off to a beach with surf lessons near Byron Bay. Unfortunately, the GPS led us to a restaurant with the same name, though nearby we found a beach with pristine waters and cool sand. It was astonishing how the British would send convicts here as a punishment. 65% of Australians were descendants of convicts.

Grand Dynasty

After the beach, we went to the only restaurant on the block, which was full—the Grand Dynasty, which had the best Chinese food I had ever tried. Our family walked around town until we found a café facing the beach. My parents had cappuccinos, and we all shared a banana bread. We arrived back at their house at around 5 p.m. I was extremely tired, but despite that, Gori, Darsh, and I still played Life. Then, at around 11 p.m., I collapsed into bed and fell fast asleep.

– *Two* –
Arrival in Port Douglas

I woke up dazed and half-awake on Wednesday morning at 6 a.m. We had to catch an early flight to Cantz. Unfortunately, as we approached the parking lot at the airport to return our rented car, my younger brother Darsh threw up. It was a $275 repair that was thankfully covered by American Express.

After going through security, we ended up in front of a sushi restaurant that also included soup, dumplings, and oversized pieces of sushi. One piece was equivalent to four pieces of sushi all in one.

Tourist tip: Do not buy food before an Australian domestic flight that is more than two hours long. Australian flights of this length serve great food on board. Of course, exceptions should be made if the food at the airport is really good.

After arriving in Cantz, our family headed to the budget desk. We rented a car and drove to Port Douglas to stay at our Airbnb. We settled down in our Airbnb when the groceries arrived. In Australia, it was a common concept that Airbnbs would be supplied with groceries. Our Airbnb was a residence among many other residences in this Airbnb community.

Snorkeling

Nonetheless, every bite of the groceries was delicious. The bread and butter were by far the best I had ever had, along with fruits and items to make the Australian breakfast, which I would call my dream breakfast. Then we all went to High

Tide, where I ordered fish and chips, and it was a decent meal.

– Three –
The Great Barrier Reef

I woke up early on Thursday, at 4 a.m. to be exact. It was 5:30 a.m., though, and I was with my family walking on the beach. Today would be a great day because we were all going to the Great Barrier Reef. Throughout our walk, more crab prints slowly appeared. At first, it was just a couple, but by the end, it seemed to be increasing dramatically. Crabs are like humans in that regard because they all wake up at different times. There were the very early birds, the early birds, and the ones that sleep in.

After the quiet walk, we returned home and had a delightful breakfast. Then we headed to our Quicksilver cruise tour. After a snack of scones with my brother, while my parents had a cappuccino (both were on sale), we set off. It was a fast and rocky ride at 40 kilometres an hour. Doing any action more than trying to stay on my two feet made me feel nauseous. Despite that, my family and I headed to a different corner of the boat. We heard a certified marine biologist speak about the Great Barrier Reef. After arriving at the reef, everyone changed into full-body suits to prevent any stings.

I was about to sign up for scuba diving when I was told by an attendant that there was a minimum age of 12. I was seven months shy of my 12th birthday. Though there was one activity I wanted to do more than scuba diving – snorkelling. I snorkelled for an hour and a half. In the middle, I had lunch from the buffet. My mum started feeling sick, though, while I was eating my lunch. The coral reef seemed to never end. It

was exactly what I had hoped for. After sending a postcard, we got back to the boat, and on our way back, I snacked on crackers and cheese. Then I fell asleep and woke up at the very end of our ride.

A car ride and a shower left our entire family at the dining table on our balcony. We ate yellow dal and rice with yoghurt, along with a couple of pieces of bread. After brushing my teeth and writing the day's recap in my journal, I was asleep before 8:30 p.m.

– Four –
Nautilus Aviation

I woke up to the rush of packing and hurrying at 6 a.m. Today, we were going to take a Nautilus Aviation tour to a private sand island in the middle of the ocean. It was a considerable distance off the coast. During the day, it served as a helicopter hangar and tourist hotspot.

How it worked was that a group of people – in this case, our family – would fly from a helicopter hangar in Cantz to the sand island. On arrival, we would be given a picnic box with champagne, sandwiches, scones and bread, along with many condiments such as very creamy butter. At the bottom were snorkelling equipment and fancy champagne glasses.

At the moment, though, we were in a rented car heading towards Cantz. After booking our tour at the reception desk, we headed next door for breakfast, where I ordered avocado toast. Soon after, we walked around downtown and grabbed a scoop of ice cream. Outside the shop, we sat down on bean bags. A helicopter flew high above us while we enjoyed our ice cream.

After finishing our ice cream, we walked around downtown again. Then my dad found an Omega store—and we were late. We rushed to our car and drove to the Natilus Aviation Centre. After signing a form, we took off, and I finally realised the hangar was right next to the airport.

Shortly after, we arrived at the sand island. The captain told us that during the night there was always a high tide, and that the island would be completely underwater. During the ride, our pilot showed us formations in the water and explained that he was from New Zealand and had moved here to fly. He also said that in two weeks he would quit this job and go over to an island nation off the coast of India, where he would fly the king's helicopters on a two-year contract.

Some time later, we were on the island with the helicopter by our side and a lunch basket beside us. Another note – according to the pilot, 95% of tourists were Chinese, so it was not surprising to see many Chinese translations. After discovering every corner of the island in five minutes, I went snorkelling and saw clear white sand everywhere I looked. After swimming, my family and I enjoyed lunch.

Time passed, and then out of nowhere, a giant rainbow appeared. Hours later, our pilot received the signal, and we returned to the centre. There I washed my feet in the shower, and then we drove home. After a shower, I collapsed in bed and fell fast asleep.

– Five –
Daintree

Our family and I had a relatively late start to the day. The jet lag was finally wearing off at last. Due to the abundance of activities we had been doing and the distance we had travelled, the jet lag had taken longer than usual to wear off.

Anyway, we quickly got out and started walking on a different beach where alligator sightings and warning signs were common. About an hour after arriving at the beach, we left. Back at our Airbnb, we enjoyed an Australian breakfast at the crack of dawn. It was an ideal breakfast for four, which included six eggs, twelve blueberry muffins, a loaf of bread, jam, and butter.

With our stomachs full, we packed our bags and headed to Daintree Forest. We parked our car at the entry centre, the starting and ending point for all tours. After receiving our tickets, we hopped on the bus, which took us to the first part of Daintree. Once there, we walked around and then came back to the bus stop. Shortly after, we were back in our car and took a ferry across a body of water. On the way, we spotted three alligators. Then we drove along a road up the Daintree.

After some time, we arrived at our first stop. It stood over the beach, and I could see mountain tops in the distance. It was no wonder that it was a very popular spot for taking photos, not to mention the dozens of islands out in the water. After taking a look around, our family got our cheese sandwiches out of the car. Shortly after the quick meal, we headed off again.

We soon arrived at a small restaurant with a great view of the beach, about forty yards away. Next to the restaurant was a trail with a sign describing an endangered species—a bird roughly the same weight as a human but slightly shorter. Though the restaurant had a nice view, there was one major activity to avoid there: eating the food. Every item except the desserts and coffee was quite mediocre, which probably explained why we were the only ones eating there. Although mediocre food might sound acceptable, it was hardly worth it considering the vast variety of great food in Australia.

Soon after, we drove to our next stop — the Daintree Ice Cream Company. All year round, they offer a sampler of three seasonal flavours. I had a yellow capote and a couple of other ice cream flavours, all of which were delicious and unlike anything I had ever tried before. My mum complimented the chef, and he even gave us a free scoop of black capote. After the unexpected treat, we all took bathroom breaks. On our drive home, my dad spotted a wine store and decided to have a couple of tastings.

After that, we were finally on our way home. Although the afternoon had gone by, our evening was just beginning.

Right after arriving back at our Airbnb, we headed off to the carnival. Unfortunately, shortly after receiving our tickets, we realised that only one activity remained, and it was for those aged fifteen and older. We then decided to go to a recommended restaurant instead. It was a nice dinner with a great dessert that took twenty minutes to bake. After plenty of window shopping — plus a purchase of two boomerangs that actually worked (I tested them later in my backyard) — we headed home for a night's rest.

– Six –

From Port Douglas to the Harbour City

I woke up early on Sunday at 7 a.m. Our family had an Australian breakfast and enjoyed every perk of the Airbnb. Then we headed to the airport for our flight to Sydney. It was a normal flight and a smooth Uber ride to our hotel. The Uber driver shared my interest in golf and cricket.

The hotel was Sofitel, and my dad had a free room upgrade and a lounge pass. The lounge on the top floor had several TVs displaying the news and offered a great view of Australia. In the morning, it served a gourmet breakfast, and for the rest of the day, it provided countless snacks — sandwiches, churros, salmon, and a variety of fruits, to name just a few. Unfortunately, children were not allowed after 5:00 p.m., though before that, they could be there without adult supervision. At least after 5:00 p.m., my parents could both enjoy a complimentary appetiser.

After some rest in our room, we went out to the square. All over Sydney, there was a festival called *Vivid*. There was a light show at the Opera House, but in this square, there was a gigantic robot, more than half the size of our hotel. It was made of plastic and performed a great seven-minute show every thirty minutes.

Soon after watching the show, we had dinner at Moti Mahal. It turns out there is a lot of history behind it — the chefs and owners are descendants of the inventor of butter chicken. Over time, they moved south to Australia, bringing the recipe with them, and once here, they opened a few restaurants. Thus, Moti Mahal was born in Australia.

Overall, it was a wonderful meal, and the butter chicken was the star of the show. After dinner, we roamed around the square for a couple of hours before returning to our room and falling fast asleep.

– Seven –
Bondi Beach

We woke up the next morning refreshed and ready. First, we all had breakfast; I had eggs Benedict — and then my family and I headed to Bondi Beach, a local favourite. Although we were in the Southern Hemisphere and it was winter, I had briefly forgotten about that while on the northeastern coast in Port Douglas, where it is summer weather all year round. Unfortunately, Sydney is on the southeastern coast, so it was rather cool. The water was relatively close to the Southern Ocean, which might explain why it was freezing cold! After our unorthodox beach visit, we grabbed lunch at a Mediterranean restaurant.

It was a quiet evening at the hotel until daylight faded and

night fell over Sydney. We headed out to the lively square; it was as loud as a concert out there. We roamed around for hours, enjoyed the robot shows, had dinner, and then returned to our room, eager for the next day.

– Eight –
Opera House

I woke up with a buzz in my step because today my family and I were going to the Opera House. We first went to the lounge, where I had poached eggs for breakfast. The Opera House was on the other side of town, so we had to take two ferries instead of the customary one.

Finally, the Sydney Harbour Bridge appeared, with the Opera House beneath it. After getting off the ferry, we walked up the stairs of the Opera House and went to the ticket desk, where we received headphones and tickets. We then went to a nearby diner for lunch before returning for the tour.

Our guide led us through all the best parts of the Opera House in about an hour. Before the tour began, we had a briefing on its history and watched a short video. I found the story behind Australia's most iconic symbol much more intriguing than I had imagined.

Any Sydney tour guide will tell a tourist that the Opera House is well known for its unique design, but few will share its origin story. It began in the early 1960s, when a panel of judges held a contest. The winner would receive $20,000 and a leadership role in designing the building.

Jørn Utzon's application was originally disqualified. However, one judge, dissatisfied with the accepted entries, decided to review the rejected ones and was impressed by Jørn's design. On the day of the announcement, the prize was awarded to the Danish architect, who was then a relatively unknown 38-year-old.

Although he became an overnight sensation, things did not end well. After a disagreement with a board member, tensions grew, and Jørn was eventually removed from his role as architect. He left Australia and never returned.

A few years later, Queen Elizabeth visited Australia to officially open the Opera House. Fortunately, Jørn was honoured and forgiven decades later.

Unfortunately, by this time, his health had deteriorated significantly, and he was unable to visit. Despite this, he still received the recognition he deserved. In 2006, Jørn Utzon became only the second architect ever to live to see one of his creations named a World Heritage Site. The first person to achieve this distinction was a Brazilian.

After the history briefing and video, we were led through the auditoriums, the theatre, and various rooms, including one where people were rehearsing for a musical.

After the tour, my family and I headed to the ticket counter. We tried to get tickets for a concert or musical in the coming days. Unfortunately, all the concerts and musicals were booked out because of the Vivid music festival. After our unsuccessful

attempt to book a night at the symbol of a continent, we took a taxi to our hotel, the Sofitel. My dad then went to an opening meeting for the conference. Over the next couple of days, he would attend several meetings and speak at many of them.

It would culminate on Saturday, with hundreds of people attending, and there would be at least a couple of dozen meetings along the way. The first one had already started, so my dad left the room and went down to the lobby. My mum, brother, and I had other plans because my mum was a doctor and would not be attending the conference.

We decided to make the most of our time in Sydney. After resting in our room for a couple of hours, we got ready to go out. My dad had a very close friend we were meeting that day. He had recently become president of ASSIP, which meant

Mum wanted us to be presentable and properly dressed.

We headed to Moti Mahal again, where we met the ASSIP president (as of June 2019) and my dad's good friend, Sudhir Diwan. The adults chatted, occasionally asking my brother and me questions. Dinner went on for hours. Feeling stuffed, I left at 11:30 p.m., half-asleep. It was a slow, noisy walk back to the Sofitel, and I fell asleep the moment I touched the bed.

– Nine –
Wild and Sea Life Sydney

It was a rather lazy start to a Wednesday morning. We had covered the top six tourist attractions in the last couple of days.

Tourist tip: do not visit the botanical garden. Although it is nice, it certainly isn't worth spending your valuable time in the world's most isolated continent to see it. I can guarantee you will find better activities to fill your time, and that there is probably a botanical garden of similar quality near you.

But that was yesterday, and this was now. We were in a lounge suspended high in the air, overlooking Darling Harbour, sitting on a couch with my brother, watching YouTube videos on my dad's phone. For the first time in days, time felt slow and heavy.

Finally, my dad came back to the lounge to take us to Wild Life Sydney. We had already visited all the intriguing, world-class monuments and tourist attractions, so, with no family in town, the quality of the attractions was going down. To make a long story short, we had seen all there was to see in Sydney.

Therefore, we went to still interesting but less incredible places. Fortunately, though, Wild Life Sydney far exceeded my expectations. It was a good place to visit considering our situation and location. The aquarium was just across the street, over the bridge.

As many experiences begin, we were at the ticket desk first. There was a full package ticket that included Wild Life and Sea Life—not to mention a celebrity-themed exhibit with another attraction about ten minutes away. Obviously, as the title shows, we were not intrigued by the celebrity-based exhibit. We might have gone to the other one if it had been much closer, rather than ten minutes away.

Finally, we were inside, where we saw small fish of all kinds. The first big stop came when we went through a transparent glass tunnel. There we saw sharks, dolphins, and most notably, a dugong—one of only four dugongs on display in the world. Its diet was entirely lettuce. The display told the story of how it had been found in terrible condition in 2001, treated, and released back into the wild, only to be discovered again on the coast of Queensland in 2003 or 2004 in even worse condition. It was then brought here, where it has lived ever since. After that, we went to a section with a transparent glass cylinder in the middle of a water body. There, we saw some more unique fish. Before long, we realised we had seen all there was to see in Sea Life. Wild Life, although less iconic,

was still a pleasant way to pass the time.

Although my interests were not closely aligned with the

displays at Sea Life, my family and I were out of there much quicker. Once outside, my mum left to attend her event while my dad stayed and introduced my brother and me to some fellow attendees and speakers at the conference. After a brief chat—mainly between the adults—we strolled through Darling Harbour and returned to where all our days in Sydney began: our hotel room at the Sofitel Sydney. It was quite a restful day, though things were about to change again very soon.

– Ten –

Arrival in Hobart, Tasmania

An incredible excitement filled the air again as we would be on an Airbus A380 to Hobart, Tasmania, today. South of it is where many expeditions to Antarctica begin. It is also where Bruny Island, south of Tasmania, lies, from which journeys to the Southern Ocean start. But that was not for now—the present was all about packing, checking, and checking again.

Hobart

Hours later, we checked into our hotel at 6:30 p.m. local time. Across the street was an ice cream shop that also served fresh fish. The fish was decent, although the ice cream was spectacular—one of the most underrated places I had visited during the trip. After much thought, we finally fell asleep in our hotel room a couple of hours later, skipping the midnight drive to see the stars. We enjoyed some much-needed rest, as tomorrow would be a day to remember.

– *Eleven* –
Bruny Island

It was a cool morning in Hobart. That morning, a rented SUV filled with my family headed towards Bruny Island. In short, it was a tourist's paradise, offering the best food and experiences. I was baffled by how it was still relatively unknown and unpopular compared to other major attractions on the continent.

On Bruny Island, they had the best tea, chocolate, and honey. Though I did not personally try the tea, the chocolate and honey were the best I had ever tasted. Never in my life had I been to a place with more than one type of honey available—there were over two dozen varieties. That, however, would be explored after the tour.

Before the tour began, we had some bread and cheese, which were again among the best I had ever had. Not to mention the wide and varied selection of cheeses. After the meal, we went on the Bruny Island Cruise, a three-hour journey that took us southward from Bruny Island to the Southern Ocean. Once there, we stayed for a while before turning around and heading back to conclude our boat ride.

Along the way, we spotted countless unique and rare living creatures, not to mention the enormous thirty-foot waves, which were great fun. Before that, we had to board the boat, listen to a brief speech, and then depart. It was already a cool day, as we were in the Southern Hemisphere during winter and off the southern coast, the coldest part of Australia. But there was no time to complain, as for nearly an hour it was forty-foot wave after forty-foot wave for our small boat. It felt like a rollercoaster, except there were no tracks—only the boat flying briefly before making a splashy landing that left every passenger soaked in no time.

Between waves, we saw flamingos, albatrosses, and other rare birds. Though the experience was wonderful, we were unfortunately unable to ride into the Southern Ocean due to unsafe weather conditions. Therefore, we could only catch a long glimpse of it before turning back towards Bruny Island.

On the way back, the crew handed out Tim Tams—a chocolate sweet that resembles a Bourbon biscuit. It is an Aussie staple found everywhere. Aside from the waves, it was a quiet ride back to Bruny Island.

Once there, my family and I were greeted with a pleasant surprise. Since we had not reached the Southern Ocean, everyone received a free three-course meal, which was delicious, along with $20 to spend in the gift shop. After enjoying our complimentary treats, we headed to the Bruny Island Chocolate Store, where all the island's chocolates were freshly supplied daily. The fudge chocolate was particularly tasty, though all of the dozen or more varieties were delightful. I sampled them all—it was a dream come true for any chocolate lover.

After spending some of our allowance in the store, we headed to the honey shop, where I sampled every type of honey available in Tasmania.

Once done, and after my parents bought a few jars, we headed out and came across a tea shop in the middle of a tea plantation. We did not make a long stop or any purchases, but my parents said the tea was of high quality, which I trust since they drink chai — a type of Indian tea — twice a day.

Afterwards, we went to the square near our hotel, where we found live music and a humongous chessboard. My brother, being a chess champ, was eager to play the life-sized game, but unfortunately, the pieces had been put away and the chessboard was closed for the night.

Anyhow, we danced and wandered around the square, had dinner, and then returned to the hotel late at night, where we went to sleep — eagerly anticipating the next day in a faraway land.

– Twelve –

Salamanca Flea Market and Return to Sydney

It was an early wake-up call to catch the Salamanca Flea Market, which is only open on Saturday mornings. The market had food from all over the world, as well as all sorts of items—from UGGs to jewellery to crêpes, Salamanca Market had it all. Best of all, it was only a two-minute walk from our hotel.

We had to be quick, as we had a flight to catch to return to the wide island again. While there, we quickly realised that bargaining skills were essential. I got a crêpe and a sausage to eat, and to finish my allowance, I bought three containers of different types of honey. Meanwhile, my dad bargained for a beautiful ruby ring and managed to bring the price down by over 25%. Not to mention, we also played a delayed game of chess, with my brother winning—as expected.

Once we were satisfied with our purchases and my parents were happy with their bargains, we checked out of our hotel and returned the rental vehicle. We then boarded a Boeing 737 to fly back to the capital of the continent.

After a long flight, we checked back into the Sofitel Sydney, where we would stay for the night. This time, we received an upgraded suite, which was spacious and even had a television in the bathroom—a rather unusual addition. After fully enjoying all the amenities of our upgraded room, we went out to Darling Harbour to see the fireworks, wander around, and finally conclude a fantastic day between two corners of the most isolated continent in the world—a symbolic last full day in the Land Down Under.

Top 5 MUST-DOS

Salamanca Market is another hidden treasure for food lovers in Tasmania. However, food is not the only thing this market has to offer. It is enjoyable for people of all interests. Food, clothing and various other items are available in a great variety here, not to mention the giant chessboard where anyone can play a life-sized game of chess. Do remember, though, that the board is closed after 8 p.m. Also, make sure to wake up early, as the market closes at 12 p.m.

Nautilus Aviation will provide an unforgettable experience worth saving for. It begins at their helicopter hangar in Cairns, where you purchase your tickets. From there, you will step outside to view Cairns International Airport before boarding a designated helicopter with headsets and a pilot. You will then take a brief flight across the Great

Barrier Reef to a private island about 40 yards wide and 100 yards long.

This island will be your residence for three hours, during which you will enjoy a gourmet lunch, followed by a swim and snorkelling. An ideal four hours well spent indeed.

#3 is the Opera House. Arguably, the most iconic symbol of a continent. It is a must-see for anyone visiting Sydney. The design is unique and innovative, while the history is phenomenally fascinating. Also, book your tickets early to catch a show, especially if you're visiting during a music festival.

Thought of as the most stunning natural feature of a continent, the Great Barrier Reef is the largest coral reef in the world. It is accessible by boat from either Cairns or Port Douglas. While there, snorkel and witness the vivid reefs nature has to offer. Try to save some pictures of the event, because you may never see a scene like it again. Perhaps take part in a few more activities before leaving the wonder that is the Great Barrier Reef.

The Bruny Island tour to the Southern Ocean is a remarkable experience that surpassed all my other adventures in Australia. On this tour, a customer is taken by boat into the

Southern Ocean. The small vessel, with a capacity of up to 30 people, offers the thrill of encountering forty-foot waves while witnessing a variety of unique and rare marine life. During my trip, I spotted albatrosses and flamingos.

At the end of the tour, visitors are free to explore the island and enjoy its abundance of excellent food—an ideal conclusion to a dreamlike day on Bruny Island. In case of bad weather, a customer may exchange their ticket for a future date or continue with the tour and receive $20 in gift shop credit along with a complimentary high-quality lunch.

All these reasons make this a must-do experience for anyone visiting Australia.

What I Wrote After Coming Back in the Summer of 2019

How It Came To Be

There are many ways you might have ended up reading this. Maybe you're my mum, looking through this writing for every little mistake. Maybe you're one of my classmates or friends who have heard me talk about it for endless hours and decided to see what it was all about. Or perhaps you're one of my mum's countless relatives—well, maybe not thousands, but you can imagine.

This is wonderful! Or maybe you're Ms Thompson, reading this because it's one of your student's books. You've really helped me with my writing—and I can't forget Mrs Brackeen or Ms Roper either.

Oh, and if that's not enough, you could be Ms McFather—actually, there's a pretty good chance you are—or Mrs Buckner. And what about Mr Vopelt? When Mr Thompson makes his dream a reality, he'll hear about it too.

Then there's Ms Vasquez, my old kindergarten teacher, who I think is highly underrated. Or perhaps you're Mrs Droskin, Mrs Bouchereau, Ms Wali, Ms Lynton, Ms Frost, Ms Plunkhien, Mrs Helwurst, or even Ms Ferstand. Maybe you're Mrs Mitchell or Mrs Kudak.

Or perhaps you're Mrs Payne, my old Chinese teacher, or my new French teacher, Mrs Conway—yes, I did forget your name at first, but I found it on my binder! Although when I give this to you, I'll certainly know your name because you'll then be my teacher.

You might also be Coach Gunter, Coach White, or one of my new Year 6 teachers by the time I hand this over. Or perhaps you're my mum's friend Vipma, who's been wondering for months what would happen next—or even her son, or her herd of dogs! (So you could be one of many dogs reading this.)

Then you might be my dad or younger brother, or one of my parents' patients, reading this among the piles of magazines in their clinic. If your doctor recommended this, don't worry—they'll take good care of you. They are Mouhua Ray and Mayank Gupta. And my brother, Darsh Gupta, is such a reader—so if history repeats itself, you won't have to worry about him.

A massive shout-out to my mum for not letting me leave this unfinished. There wouldn't be a book without her—literally, no exaggeration, it's true.

Oh, and here's a mention to all my Year 5 classmates and all the remarkable ones I remember—or see in the yearbooks.

If you know me or have met me, ask to be included in the next book! So, if you're a classmate, a friend, or even just a stranger looking for something to read to cure your reading block, join me as I tell you about my journey across the globe.

So how did I end up halfway across the world, in somebody's house I'd never met before—with a lead pencil, a mechanical pencil, and a pen?

Carrying an old notebook around with my mum, dad, and brother beside me—well, this is that story. But to truly understand it, we must go back to April 2018. Thirteen months prior, we were in New York City. As you may know, we live in Kansas City now.

It was the World Congress of Pain. As you can guess, my parents are pain management specialists. My dad had a speech on a study he did a couple of years earlier about curing pain caused by a stimulator injection. He was then invited to the 14th International World Congress of Pain, which was held in Sydney, Australia.

Thus began our 27-hour journey from Kansas City International Airport (MCI) to Sydney International Airport (SYD). The trip took us through five different airlines, six stops, three lounges, three cars, two hotels, two Airbnbs, and eight flights—and even a carnival—all within fifteen days.

For me, though, it was the single flight on a Boeing 787 from Los Angeles International Airport (LAX) to Brisbane International Airport that stood out. For those who don't know, I have a huge fascination with aviation—how it maintains such a strong safety record despite having so many employees and passengers. How can everything run so smoothly when an average worker reports just 90 minutes before departure? How do they keep everyone so attentive every single day for years?

After sleeping for around 17–18 hours on the flight (which is extremely rare unless you're good at sleeping on planes), we arrived feeling fresh and excited as ever. Once we placed our bags in our rental car, everyone wanted to get straight into exploring so that we could fit in an extra night. We weren't tired at all, surprisingly, thanks to that long sleep on the plane.

We only had two days in Brisbane, especially since one of them would be spent at the Gold Coast. Brisbane is an average-sized city, about 6,000 square miles, but its airport is extremely busy because it's the gateway to the Gold Coast—a top tourist destination in Australia. You might wonder how it became so popular and what will happen to Gold Coast Airport as a result. Well, I don't really know—probably because not many people realise there is a Gold Coast Airport!

I had three things in mind for Brisbane: the Story Bridge, the Koala Sanctuary, and the best one of all—Moreton Island. It's about a 40-minute drive away and is the third-largest sand island in the world.

As you may know, my parents tend to spend less on some things and more on others. Why is that important? Because my dad was saving up for the Roadster, a Tesla car that was supposed to break all major records and be released in 2020. We travel a lot as a family because we all share a huge passion for it. Our hobbies might seem normal, but when you look closer, there's always something vivid and different about the way we do things.

So, you're probably eager to get to the Australia part—so here it is.

Rushing action 3, 2, 1, go!

But my mum insisted, and Mum always makes sure I take my kid to the same places she did. She says that since she made all the effort to have us travel all over the globe, it is only fair that I do the same in return. It would be unfair not to let my child see those great places, too. Everybody should have the chance to see and experience such things.

So my view might change drastically, and it probably will by the time I have seen more of the world. Until then, this is how I see it, unless you can convince me otherwise.

We went to Queen Street Mall, where my mum and some of her old friends had been 25 years ago. Soon enough, they were chatting like old best friends. While they caught up, we looked for breakfast — boiled eggs and cereals. The kids ate quickly, while Dad and I wolfed ours down like savages.

After about two hours, we decided to go to the Koala Sanctuary. It was time to see the animals, especially the koalas. Hugging a koala costs $25 per person, which was the same as the entry fee for the entire zoo. So in total, it cost us around $100 AUD, which was quite expensive considering that half the animals were asleep and barely fed. Many were kept in small enclosures, and a crying baby nearby made the visit even less enjoyable.

If you want a better zoo experience, I would honestly suggest visiting your local zoo. It will likely be cheaper and just as good. Still, hugging a koala was a special experience, priceless to a certain extent.

My brother and I went straight to get our tickets and joined the line. His photo turned out great; he looked like he was holding the koala naturally. I was nervous as the koala was heavier than I expected, and my nerves made it even harder to hold. It probably showed, but the photo turned out fine in the end.

After collecting our photos from the café, we bought kangaroo food to feed them, but the kangaroos were too lazy to come over. After sneaking around for fifteen minutes, we realised it was not worth the time. You can find many better zoos without flying 27 hours just to see the same thing. It is simply not worth spending your valuable holiday money that way.

Next, we went to Story Bridge. My parents did not want to climb it, and my brother could not because of age restrictions. To me, it looked treacherous and even horrifying, especially for kids. Just thinking about it sent a shiver down my spine. I decided to face my fear, though, and afterwards, we settled down to eat at The Pician at Coulson House.

My brother and I had fish and chips. He is much taller than I am, and people often ask if he is older. There were only two other people there, who seemed like locals. Australia, as I found out, is not exactly the most child-friendly place on the planet.

Later, something odd happened. A man muttered something unpleasant, and my brother joked about it to my parents. I told on him, but he got away unnoticed, completely unbothered by what had happened.

After dinner, we walked around for a while but soon realised we had seen all that Brisbane had to offer. We headed to our car, paid the parking fee, and drove home. My brother and I dozed off soon after, knowing that tomorrow would be another long day.

Journal Entry: July 14 2025, 10:49 p.m.

It has been six years since that memorable trip to the Land Down Under. I am now a rising senior at Pembroke Hill instead of The Barstow School. I still play plenty of golf and hope to do so for as long as I can. The Australia trip remains close to my heart as my favourite ever journey. I still fondly remember it all — from the floor-of-lava games in Brisbane to the Opera House in Sydney.

Since then, I have been fortunate enough to travel to many countries, play lots of golf, and enjoy delicious food — I suppose some things will never change.

I have been inspired by travel journals such as *Lonely Planet* and *Fodor's Travel Guides*. I try to write a journal every day when I travel overseas. I have visited the Galápagos Islands on an educational mission, spent time with locals in remote Indian villages, and also travelled as a regular tourist. Travel is a big part of my learning, and I hope this book will encourage children to dream, learn, and share their experiences through similar travel journals and blogs.

My last trip was to Japan, where I visited Tokyo, Kyoto, Osaka, and the Okinawa Islands. I hope to write about it one day.

Please visit **kansasopinions.com** to read some of the blogs I have written over the past seven years, and feel free to share your feedback for my next work.